P9-DZN-098

The Creative Hostess OXFORD COOKBOOK

We would like to thank all those who have helped us in the preparation of this book, particularly:
Malcolm Graham, Local History Librarian, Oxfordshire County Libraries and the restaurateurs and chefs on pages 61-3 who have so kindly provided us with recipes.

TOM TOWER *(back cover)* Sir Christopher Wren's tower at Christ Church is named after the huge bell it houses. Weighing over six tons, "Great Tom" chimes 101 times every night at 9.05 p.m. during the university term, a tradition which dates back to the curfew for the 101 members of the college. Latecomers had to pay gate money.

"The clever men at Oxford
Know all that there is to be knowed.
But they none of them know one half as much
As intelligent Mr Toad."

The Wind in the Willows
KENNETH GRAHAME, 1859-1932

THE MORRIS OXFORD *(previous page)* was the first model to come out of William Morris's factory at Cowley in 1913.

First published 1981 by
Marion Edwards Limited,
10 Barley Mow Passage,
London W4.

Printed in England by
T.J. Press (Padstow) Ltd.
ISBN 0 904330 83 4
Second Impression, February 1982

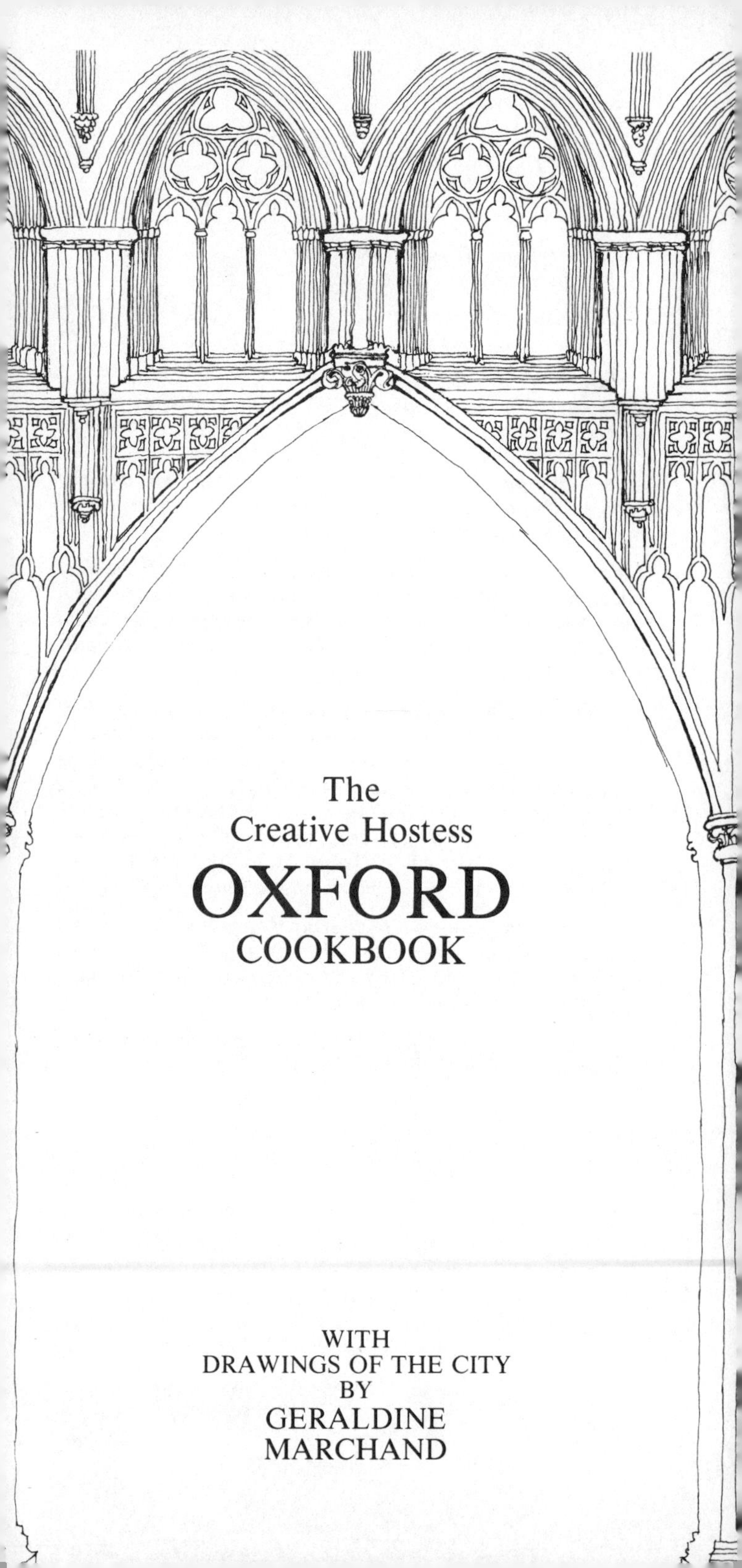

The Creative Hostess OXFORD COOKBOOK

WITH
DRAWINGS OF THE CITY
BY
GERALDINE
MARCHAND

Introduction

"So poetry, which is in Oxford made
An art, in London only is a trade."

Prologue to the University of Oxford
JOHN DRYDEN, 1631-1700

Who can fail to be impressed, when visiting Oxford, by the visible and outward signs of a lifestyle which clearly matches its surroundings? It is evident that beneath the City's "dreaming spires" may be found both eminent and aspiring scholars engrossed in the pursuit of excellence in their own particular fields.

Students of good food will happily discover that the City contains more than one culinary genius as well — for although the restaurants of Oxford are varied in style, price range and cuisine, there are several which share the same high standards and an obvious desire to please.

So that you may further enjoy all that Oxford has to offer, these creative chefs have kindly provided us with a selection of their favourite recipes. Some are traditionally English, while others come from what were once referred to as "the far-flung outposts of the Empire"! They reflect our history, a cosmopolitan college population and, above all, our varied diet today. (Like all great cities, Oxford has one foot in the past, one in the present, and its sights on the future.)

In this small volume are outstanding recipes from the culinary masters of Oxford, together with a taste of the town in the form of specially commissioned drawings and a bouquet garni *of interesting facts and legends.*

Join us on a visit to Oxford, and share with us the secrets and specialities of its leading chefs.

"I can't see who's ahead — it's either Oxford or Cambridge."

JOHN SNAGGE BBC Commentary on the Boat Race, 1949

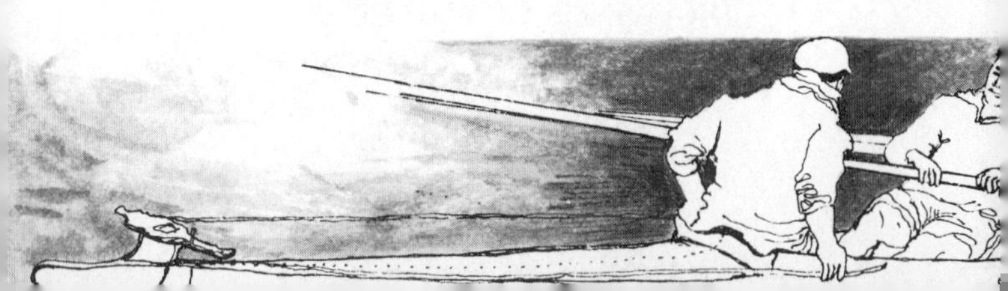

Contents

A note on measures and conversions
Ingredients are given in metric, Imperial and American measures. **Use measures from one column only**. Teaspoon and tablespoon measures in the metric column correspond to 5 ml and 15 ml respectively.

Matthew Arnold described Oxford poetically as "that sweet city with her dreaming spires", but beneath Oxford's beauty has ever lain the iron hand of power enclosed in a velvet glove. As early as the year 912 it was reported that "King Edward took possession of London and Oxford, and of all the lands which owed obedience thereto." But in more recent years its power has relied more subtly upon the influential men and women who have passed through its college doors.

For what would, at first sight, appear to be a seat of learning rooted in the Establishment, Oxford can boast academic sons and daughters of a remarkably wide political spectrum. Famous sons range from Anthony Eden to Jo Grimond to Harold Wilson, while among its daughters it numbers Margaret Thatcher, Shirley Williams and Barbara Castle!

The birth of Oxford

But how did it all begin? The answer lies quite simply in the City's name: Oxford was sited on an ancient ford of the river Thames across which oxen could be driven. If the City's coat of arms depicting an ox crossing a stream seems familiar, it is probably because any reader over the age of thirty would have been used to seeing this crest proudly displayed on (pre British Leyland) Morris motor-cars.

Young man makes good

The Morris story began before the turn of the century when young William opened a small bicycle shop in Oxford. His enthusiasm for "the horseless carriage" led him to design and build the Morris Oxford in 1913, the first model to come out of his factory at Cowley, a suburb of Oxford. In a very few years he had risen to fame and fortune, becoming a peer in 1934. He showed his gratitude to the City for its part in his success by giving large donations to Oxford hospitals and founding Nuffield College, named after him.

RADCLIFFE CAMERA

After Dr John Radcliffe, physician to Queen Anne, had left £40,000 in his will for the building of a library, it took twenty years' negotiating to clear the site of buildings. The Radcliffe Camera was finally built in 1749. Originally a science library, it is now a reading room of the Bodleian, to which it is joined by a tunnel. A conveyor belt carries books between the Old Library and the New Library.

The University

The University was granted a papal ordinance in 1214. At this time there were no colleges as such — students lived in private lodgings and lectures took place in hired halls. A combination of high rents and rowdy student behaviour led to a spectacular battle between the people of Oxford and the students on St Scholastica's Day, 1355. It is reported that the citizens responded to the bell of St Martin at Carfax, while students rallied to the tolling of the bell of University Church in the High Street. Those concerned with modern day media reports of youthful disruptions may take some comfort from the knowledge that it has all happened before! Having the backing of both Church and King, the University not surprisingly won the day, and thereafter controlled rents, weights and

Continued on page 10...

MERTON COLLEGE, MOB QUAD

It is generally thought that "Mob quad" is the oldest college quadrangle in England, though its square shape is the result of gradual additions during the fourteenth century rather than deliberate design.

Continued from page 7...
measures and the discipline of scholars and townspeople alike. The University's extraordinary powers — at least in theory — continued until the nineteenth century.

Because books and reading materials were expensive, up to the eighteenth century oral examination was the order of the day, but by this time it had degenerated to farcical standards. It is said that Lord Eldon's final examination for a BA degree in Hebrew and History consisted of two questions: "What is the Hebrew for the place of a skull" and "Who founded University College?" to which Eldon replied "Golgotha" and "Alfred the Great".

One remaining relic of ancient habits is that of wearing gowns. Undergraduates normally wear short ones, the privilege of a long gown being reserved for scholars and exhibitioners.

Extracurricular activities

As well as "reading" their chosen subject preparatory to taking lengthy written examinations, today's undergraduates are encouraged to partake in a wide variety of extracurricular activities. To gain a "Blue" for representing the University in a sport is considered by some students as important as gaining a degree! Another prestigious achievement is to become President of the Union. The Oxford Union Society was founded in 1823, and former Presidents include William Gladstone, Lord Salisbury, Lord Birkenhead and Harold Macmillan.

A seat of learning

Currently, undergraduates are likely to enter the University at 18 or 19 for a three-year period. This contrasts with the first students who entered the University at 15 or 16, and spent seven years covering a wide variety of subjects from rhetoric to astronomy. But the objective remains the same — that the young people who pass through its doors shall go out into the world with the ability to blaze trails, lead people and enhance the arts.

Keats wrote "Beauty is truth, truth beauty": in the fair City of Oxford may be found a meeting of matter and minds which successfully combines the two.

CARFAX TOWER CLOCK

At Carfax — the crossroads that has always marked the centre of Oxford and takes its name from the French *carrefour* — is the fourteenth century tower that was once part of St Martin's church. You can watch the "quarter boys" strike their bells every fifteen minutes.

MUNCHY MUNCHY SALAD DIP

Serves 8

A variety of fresh fruits and vegetables is used in this crunchy starter from this popular Malaysian restaurant. Select your fruits and vegetables carefully to ensure you have a pleasing variety of colours. Choose from Granny Smith apples, fresh pineapple, mandarin segments, mango (on the raw side), fresh bean-shoots, cucumber and shredded white cabbage. Serve with some fried prawn crackers and potato crisps.

1. Wash and cut the vegetables and fruits into bite-size pieces and arrange on plates.
2. Arrange the prawn crackers and potato crisps in a bowl.

For the dip you will need:

Metric		*lb/oz*	*U.S.A.*
1 tbsp	*Fresh chilli*	1 tbsp	1 tbsp
	or		
1 tsp	*Dried chilli*	1 tsp	1 tsp
250 g	*Freshly roasted peanuts*	8 oz	2 cups
1 tbsp	*Terasi (or Blachan) powder*	1 tbsp	1 tbsp
150 ml	*Vegetable oil*	¼ cup	½ cup
2 tbsp	*Brown sugar*	2 tbsp	3 tbsp
1	*Lemon, squeezed* or	1	1
2 tbsp	*Tamarind juice 'Assam'*	2 tbsp	3 tbsp
1 tsp	*Salt*	1 tsp	1 tsp

1. Soak chilli (if dried) in hot water for 30 minutes. Drain.
2. Place the peanuts and terasi in foil in a moderate oven, 180°C, 350°F, Gas Mark 4, for 20 minutes.
3. Remove and place in a blender with the chilli and oil. Add the sugar, tamarind juice and salt and blend well.
4. Place in a bowl and serve with the fruit and vegetables.

MAGDALEN COLLEGE BELLTOWER AND BRIDGE

The bells of Magdalen announce the return of spring at 6 a.m. on Mayday morning, when a choir sings a *Te Deum* from the top of the tower.

Founded by Wayneflete, Bishop of Winchester, in 1458 for the study of theology and philosophy, Magdalen was the wealthiest foundation in Oxford and remains one of the three richest colleges today.

CHICKEN AND WALNUT PATE

Serves 6-8

The chef of Ladbroke Linton Lodge has given us his recipe for this delicious and simple-to-make pâté.

Metric		*lb/oz*	*U.S.A.*
250 g	*Chicken livers*	8 oz	8 oz
50 g	*Butter*	2 oz	¼ cup
¼	*Onion, diced*	¼	¼
1	*Garlic clove, crushed*	1	1
4	*Streaky bacon rashers, chopped*	4	4
2	*Bay leaves*	2	2
1 tbsp	*Brandy*	1 tbsp	1 tbsp
2 tbsp	*Sherry*	2 tbsp	2 tbsp
1	*Egg, large*	1	1
4 tbsp	*Walnuts, chopped*	4 tbsp	6 tbsp

1. Melt the butter in a pan, add chicken livers, diced onion, garlic, bacon and bay leaves. Cook for 5-10 minutes. Leave to cool and remove the bay leaves.
2. Mince the mixture (or chop finely) and put into a mixing bowl. Add the brandy, sherry, egg, walnuts and season to taste. Mix well.
3. Spread the mixture into an ungreased ovenproof dish.
4. Place the dish in a roasting tin half filled with hot water, and bake at 170°C, 325°F, Gas Mark 3 for 1 hour. Cool before serving.

NOSEBAG SALAD

Serves 4 as a side salad

This deliciously crunchy salad ranks high in the popularity ratings of the many salads served in the Nosebag Restaurant. The basic mix is given below but don't be afraid to adjust quantities to your personal taste.

Metric		*lb/oz*	*U.S.A.*
1 can	*Sweetcorn (600 g, 20 oz)*	1 can	1 can
125 g	*Salted peanuts*	4 oz	1 cup
125 g	*Cucumber*	4 oz	4 oz
	Red and green pepper		
	Mustard and cress to taste		
	Olives to taste		

1. Drain the corn and place in a large bowl with the peanuts.
2. Peel the cucumber, cut to quarters lengthwise then into 2 cm (1") chunks, and stir in.
3. Finely slice the red and green peppers and add with the cress and olives to taste.

Next to the river is the Botanic Garden, the oldest in England, founded in connection with the Faculty of Medicine in 1621.

GATEAU DE TOPINAMBOURS AU COULIS D'ASPERGES
JERUSALEM ARTICHOKE MOUSSE WITH ASPARAGUS SAUCE

Serves 8

Monsieur Blanc has established, in a short time, an international reputation for his Quat' Saisons restaurant. He has contributed his recipe for this unusual starter.

Metric		*lb/oz*	*U.S.A.*
2 kg	*Jerusalem artichokes*	4 lb	4 lb
3	*Eggs, whole*	3	3
3	*Eggs, yolks only*	3	3
750 ml	*Whipping or double cream*	1 ¼ pt	2 ½ cups
½	*Lemon, squeezed*	½	½
1 tbsp	*Clarified butter*	1 tbsp	1 tbsp
1 kg	*Green asparagus**	2 lb	2 lb
150 ml	*Chicken stock*	¼ pt	½ cup
25 g	*Chervil*	14 sprigs	14 sprigs
125 g	*Butter*	4 oz	½ cup

1. Boil the artichokes gently for 20 minutes then remove the skins. Dry in a low oven to remove any excess moisture, then place in a liquidiser and blend.
2. Add the eggs, yolks, 600 ml (1 pt, 2 cups) of the cream and the lemon juice to the liquidiser and blend on a slow speed for two minutes. Season to taste, re-blend briefly and pass through a fine strainer.
3. Brush the insides of eight ramekin dishes with melted clarified butter and refrigerate until set. When set, pour in the artichoke mixture and place the ramekins in a bain marie (a roasting tin containing 2 cm, 1", hot water) and bake in the middle of the oven at 175°C, 350°F, Gas Mark 3, for 40 minutes.
4. To make the sauce, trim the asparagus, blanch for five minutes*, then cool under water. Reserve eight spears.
5. Place the chicken stock in a saucepan with the chervil. Bring to the boil then remove from the heat and leave to stand for 10 minutes to infuse. Add the asparagus, pour into a liquidiser and blend until smooth. Add the remaining cream, season to taste. Blend for 2 minutes until smooth and creamy, then force through a fine strainer into a casserole; bring to the boil. Away from the heat, work in the remaining butter and keep warm.
6. When the artichoke mousses are cooked, turn them out on to a warm deep dish. Place the 8 reserved asparagus spears in a decorative manner on top of the mousses and pour the asparagus sauce around them. Serve immediately.

**This is the very thin "grass" asparagus. If only thicker stalks are available, longer cooking time will be required — Editor.*

THE HOUSE OF COMMONS met in the University's parliament house, Convocation House, during the Plague of London. It still has no artificial lighting.

MARKET

This covered marketplace is entered from Market Street and "the High". Here you can buy everything from meat to hardware.

SPICY SKEWERED PRAWN BALLS *Serves 4*

You will need to visit a Chinese supermarket if you want to include *all* the ingredients in this recipe for Saté Udang from Munchy Munchy: once they are obtained, it is a quick and easy starter.

Metric		*lb/oz*	*U.S.A.*
500 g	*King prawns, shelled and de-veined*	1 lb	1 lb
2 tbsp	*Peanut oil*	2 tbsp	2 tbsp
	For the seasoning:		
50 g	*Coconut cream*	2 oz	2 oz
125 g	*Ground almonds*	4 oz	½ cup
1	*Garlic clove, crushed*	1	1
1 tsp	*Chilli, ground*	1 tsp	1 tsp
1	*Lemon, rind and juice*	1	1
2 tbsp	*Brown sugar*	2 tbsp	3 tbsp
1 tsp	*Terasi powder (Blachan), optional*	1 tsp	1 tsp

1. Place all the seasoning ingredients in a bowl with 4 tbsp water and 1 tsp salt and mix well.
2. Brush the king prawns with the seasoning and thread them on to skewers.
3. Place under a hot grill or barbecue them over an open fire. Brush with peanut oil and turn frequently, cooking for 3-5 minutes on each side. Serve with a plate of fresh salad.

PAUPIETTES DE SOLE "ST PIERRE"
SOLE WITH PRAWN AND VERMOUTH SAUCE — *Serves 4*

A rich and creamy fish starter contributed by Mr J. Geoghegan of Wren's.

Metric		*lb/oz*	*U.S.A.*
	2 × 400 g (14 oz) Lemon or Dover soles, filleted		
1	*Lemon, juice of*	1	1
16	*Large prawns in the shell*	16	16
250 g	*White fish*	8 oz	8 oz
300 ml	*Whipping or double cream*	½ pt	1 cup
2	*Fresh chervil sprigs*	2	2
125 ml	*Dry white vermouth*	3 fl oz	⅓ cup
2	*Shallots, finely chopped*	2	2
50 g	*Mushrooms, finely sliced*	2 oz	½ cup
10 g	*Butter*	¼ oz	2 tsp
1	*Egg yolk*	1	1

1. Sprinkle the fillets with lemon juice and gently cross-cut to prevent shrinkage. Refrigerate for 30 minutes.
2. Shell half the prawns and remove the tract from them all. Reserve the unshelled prawns for garnishing. Place the white fish in a liquidiser with the shelled prawns and blend. Slowly add half the cream and a sprig of chervil. Season to taste with salt and fine white pepper, and liquidise until very smooth. Chill in the refrigerator.
3. Flatten the fillets on a board and spread with the chilled mixture. Place one fillet on top of another, the filling on both uppermost, and roll gently into a mini "Swiss-roll". Secure with a cocktail stick and place in an ovenproof dish. Repeat with the remaining fillets.
4. Cover the rolls with vermouth and add the shallots and mushrooms. Season to taste, then cover the dish with foil. Cook at 200°C, 400°F, Gas Mark 6 for 15-20 minutes.
5. Remove, and strain the cooking liquid into a saucepan. Bring to the boil and cook until the liquid is reduced by half. Add the remainder of the cream and boil merrily! Add the butter, then take the pan off the heat and whisk in the egg yolk. Carefully lift the rolls on to a warmed serving plate, coat with sauce and garnish with the reserved prawns and chervil.

TERRINE DE TROIS POISSONS AU BEURRE BLANC
MOUSSELINE OF WHITING *Serves 10*

A delectable combination from Wren's Restaurant.

Metric		*lb/oz*	*U.S.A.*
1.25 kg	*White fish (half whiting, half lemon sole), boned and skinned*	2½ lb	2½ lb
125 g	*Salmon, raw*	4 oz	4 oz
½	*Lemon, squeezed*	½	½
50 g	*Parsley, finely chopped*	2 oz	½ cup
1	*Cayenne pepper, pinch of*	1	1
1	*Egg white*	1	1
700 ml	*Whipping cream*	1¼ pt	2½ cups
1	*Ricard, dash of*	1	1
	For the sauce:		
150 ml	*White wine*	¼ pt	½ cup
50 g	*Shallots or small onions, chopped*	2 ozs	½ cup
1 tbsp	*Pepper*	1 tbsp	1 tbsp
2 tbsp	*Cream for sauce (optional)*	2 tbsp	2 tbsp
250 g	*Unsalted butter*	8 oz	1 cup
	For the garnish:		
125 g	*Puff pastry trimmings or frozen puff pastry*	4 oz	4 oz
	Milk or beaten egg for glaze		
	Lettuce or watercress		

1. Wash and fillet the fish and cut up into cubes. Cut the salmon into 5 cm (2") wide strips and place in a bowl with the lemon juice for 10 minutes. Season with salt, pepper, parsley and cayenne pepper.
2. Liquidise the white fish until smooth. Add the egg white and blend for 2 minutes more. Refrigerate for an hour.
3. Return to liquidiser and blend in cream and Ricard.
4. Lightly butter a terrine or loaf tin and line the walls and base with the fish purée. Lay several strips of salmon on top, then cover with more fish mixture. Continue until full, smooth off the top, cover with oiled tin foil. Return to the refrigerator for an hour.
5. Preheat the oven to 200°C, 400°F, Gas Mark 6. Half fill a roasting tin with hot water. Place the terrine in it, making sure the water comes well up the side. Cook on the middle shelf for 50 minutes. Set aside to cool slightly*.
6. To make a sauce, place the wine in a saucepan with the shallots and pepper, boil until reduced by half, then transfer the mixture to a jug or bowl and pass through a

"Will you walk a little faster? said a whiting to a snail.
There's a porpoise close behing us, and he's treading
on my tail."

Alice in Wonderland
LEWIS CARROLL, 1832-1898

sieve back into the saucepan over a gentle heat. (Stir in the cream, if liked.) Whisk in the butter.

7. Use left-over puff pastry trimmings (or a small amount of frozen pastry) to make "fleurons". Roll out on a floured board and press out crescent shapes with a circular cutter. Make a criss-cross pattern on top with a sharp knife, and glaze with a little milk or beaten egg. Place on a damp baking tray in a preheated oven, 200°C, 400°F, Gas Mark 6, for about 10 minutes.
8. To serve, either present the mousseline in the terrine or de-mould on to a warmed platter and slice. Cover with the sauce, surround with fleurons and garnish with watercress.

**This terrine can also be served cold with tomato salad — Editor.*

FROGS' LEGS WITH CREAM AND CHIVES *Serves 6*

Leap over this one if you must, but bear in mind that it's tasty enough to turn the dullest of guests into Prince Charming! The recipe comes from the Randolph Hotel.

Metric		*lb/oz*	*U.S.A.*
500 g	*Frogs' legs*	1 lb	1 lb
¼ bott	*Dry white wine*	¼ bott	¼ bott
1	*Bay leaf*	1	1
6	*Black peppercorns*	6	6
1	*Lemon*	1	1
300 ml	*Double cream*	½ pt	1 cup
	Chives to taste		
	To garnish:		
	Lettuce, tomato and parsley sprigs		

1. Place the frogs' legs in a pan with the wine, bay leaf, peppercorns and half the lemon. Add cold water to cover.
2. Bring rapidly to the boil, simmer for one minute and take off the heat. Cool the legs in the cooking liquor then chill.
3. Squeeze juice from remaining half lemon into the cream, season and leave to "sour". Add chives to the cream.
4. Arrange the legs on the lettuce leaves and coat with the dressing, tomato and cut into "fans" and parsley sprigs.

Oliver Cromwell was Chancellor of the University, and Christ Church numbers **thirteen British Prime Ministers** among its famous members.

Among today's leading British politicians are an amazing number of Oxford graduates of all political persuasions: **Sir Harold Macmillan** (Balliol), **Edward Heath** (Balliol), **Margaret Thatcher** (Somerville), and **Lord Hailsham** (All Souls) all studied at Oxford. But so did **Jo Grimond** (Balliol), **Sir Harold Wilson** (Jesus), **Barbara Castle** (St Hugh's), **Michael Foot** (Wadham) ... *and* **Shirley Williams** (Somerville), co-founder of our newest political party.

Cardinal Wolsey was a fellow of Magdalen, while **Cardinal Newman** attended Trinity. Christ Church can claim **John Wesley**, and **Archbishop Laud** is buried in St John's chapel.

THE INTERNATIONAL CONNECTION

Christ Church numbers **eleven Governors-General of India** among its graduates, together with **William Penn** founder of Pennsylvania, while Corpus Christi can claim the founder of the American State of Georgia **General Oglethorpe**.

From St Peter's came **Carl Albert** Speaker of the U.S. House of Representatives, and from Trinity **George Calvert** founder of Maryland. Balliol lists the **King of Norway** among its past students. In the post-war political arena, St John's counts among former students **Lester Pearson**, Canadian Prime Minister, and **Dean Rusk**, U.S. Secretary of State.

WRITERS AND POETS

Aldous Huxley, **Matthew Arnold** and **Graham Greene** are all Balliol men while St John's graduates include **Robert Graves** and **Kingsley Amis**. Among Somerville famous members are **Dorothy Sayers**, **Vera Brittain** and **Iris Murdoch**.

Christ Church was the academic home of **Sir Philip Sidney**, **C.L. Dodgson** (**Lewis Carroll** of Alice fame) and

BODLEIAN LIBRARY CEILING *(left)*

This elaborately painted ceiling, completed in 1612, is in the oldest part of the library. Each panel shows the university arms and between each is Sir Thomas Bodley's coat of arms.

W.H. Auden, while **Oscar Wilde, C.S. Lewis** and **Sir John Betjeman** the Poet Laureate, all went to Magdalen. **J.R.R. Tolkien**, on the other hand, was at Exeter and **Stephen Spender** at University College.

T.S. Eliot, Angus Wilson and **Sir Max Beerbohm** are all Merton men, while **John Galsworthy, A.P. Herbert** and **John Fowles** all passed through the doors of New College. From Brasenose came **John Buchan** and **William Golding**, and from Trinity **Terence Rattigan. Lady Elizabeth Longford** and **Lady Antonia Fraser** are both graduates of Lady Margaret Hall.

MUSICIANS, ARTISTS AND ARCHITECTS

Sir William Walton, whose composition Crown Imperial was a part of the musical wedding service of the Prince and Princess of Wales, graduated from Christ Church, while the conductors **Sir Thomas Beecham** and **Sir Adrian Boult** studied at Wadham and Christ Church respectively. **Leopold Stokowski** was at Queen's.

The artist and designer **William Morris** was at Exeter, while **Sir Christopher Wren** the architect of St Paul's Cathedral, is associated with both Wadham and All Souls.

SCIENTISTS, SOLDIERS, EXPLORERS

Edmund Halley (of comet fame) was at Queen's, and biologist **Julian Huxley** at Balliol.

Sir Walter Raleigh and **Cecil Rhodes** benefactor of Rhodes Scholarships and founder of Rhodesia (now Zimbabwe), were both at Oriel, and **Earl Haig** at Brasenose. A famous graduate of Jesus was **T.E. Lawrence**, known as **Lawrence of Arabia**.

LET US NOT OVERLOOK...

Richard "Beau" Nash the Georgian leader of fashion who was at Jesus, and **Thomas Arnold** the Headmaster of Rugby School immortalised in "Tom Brown's Schooldays", studied at Corpus Christi and was a Fellow of Oriel.

And, last but not least, spare a thought for **Samuel Johnson**, whose teapot is displayed in the Senior Common Room at Pembroke, who was forced to leave after only a year for lack of funds!

SCHOOLS QUADRANGLE

This outstanding Perpendicular stonework fronts the Divinity School and Bodleian Library. Sir Thomas Bodley started stocking the library from scratch in 1598. Four years later, he had acquired two thousand volumes. The fact that they now number over two million owes something to his ability in persuading the Stationers' Company which controlled the output of books, that they would send the library a free copy of every book printed in England.

STEAK, GUINNESS AND MUSHROOM PIE *Serves 6*

A traditional British recipe from Browns Restaurant.

Metric		*lb/oz*	*U.S.A.*
500 g	*Stewing steak, cubed*	1 lb	1 lb
300 ml	*Guinness*	½ pt	1 cup
1	*Mixed herbs, pinch of*	1	1
1 tbsp	*Granulated sugar*	1 tbsp	1 tbsp
1 tbsp	*Worcestershire sauce*	1 tbsp	1 tbsp
2	*Bay leaves*	2	2
100 g	*Mushrooms, quartered*	4 oz	1 cup
1	*Large onion, chopped*	1	1
1	*Large carrot, sliced*	1	1
1	*Celery stick, chopped*	1	1
2 tbsp	*Tomato purée*	2 tbsp	2 tbsp
1	*Beef stock cube*	1	1
500 g	*Puff pastry*	1 lb	1 lb
1	*Egg, beaten*	1	1

1. Put the steak, Guinness, herbs, sugar, Worcestershire sauce and bay leaves into a large pan. Season with salt and pepper. (If the meat is not covered, add a little water.) Bring to the boil and simmer until the meat is tender.
2. Add the vegetables and bring back to the boil. Simmer until they are tender. Add the tomato purée and stock cube. Bring back to the boil and remove from the stove.
3. Put the mixture into a large pie dish or six small ones.
4. Cover with pastry, and decorate with pastry "leaves". Brush with egg and place in a hot oven, 220°C, 425°F, Gas Mark 7, for 20 minutes until golden brown.

SHAKESPEARE stayed at 3 Cornmarket Street, then an inn, en route from Stratford to London. It was owned by the Davenants, and Shakespeare was godfather to their son.

PARSONAGE GOLDEN STEAK *Serves 4*

An easy but delicious way to serve steak from the Old Parsonage Hotel.

Metric		*lb/oz*	*U.S.A.*
	4 × 250 g (8 oz) Sirloin steaks		
3 tbsp	*French mustard*	3 tbsp	4 tbsp
3 tbsp	*Demerara sugar*	3 tbsp	4 tbsp
50 g	*Butter*	2 oz	¼ cup
250 g	*Button mushrooms*	8 oz	2 cups
2	*Tomatoes, halved*	2	2
8	*Watercress sprigs*	8	8

1. Grill the steak under a high heat until just underdone.
2. Remove from the heat and coat with French mustard and demerara sugar.
3. Grill until the mustard and sugar are sizzling.
4. Remove from the grill and place on a warm serving dish.
5. Melt the butter in a pan and add the mushrooms. Cook gently for a few minutes then place on the plate with the steaks. Garnish with tomatoes and watercress.

"In proceeding to the dining room the gentleman gives one arm to the lady he escorts — it is unusual to offer both." LEWIS CARROLL, 1832-1898

MUNCHY MUNCHY HAMBURGERS *Serves 6*

A quick and easy way to add a spicy touch to an everyday dish. The restaurant serve theirs with chilli sauce.

Metric		*lb/oz*	*U.S.A.*
500 g	*Minced beef*	1 lb	1 lb
6	*Garlic cloves, crushed*	6	6
6 tsp	*Cornflour*	6 tsp	6 tsp
2 tbsp	*Dark soya sauce*	2 tbsp	3 tbsp
2 tbsp	*Brown sugar*	2 tbsp	2 tbsp
1 tsp	*Nutmeg, ground*	1 tsp	1 tsp
3	*Eggs, medium sized, beaten*	3	3
	Oil for frying		
2	*Large onions, sliced thickly*	2	2
6	*Sesame buns*	6	6
4	*Raw onion rings*	4	4

1. Mix together the steak, garlic, cornflour, soya sauce, sugar, nutmeg and egg. Season to taste.
2. Divide the mixture into six portions. Roll into balls, flatten and grill on a hot griddle or fry in an oiled pan.
3. At the same time, fry the onions in another pan.
4. Toast the buns on both sides. Top hamburgers with fried onions, enclose in the buns, and top with onion rings.

THE SHELDONIAN THEATRE

The Sheldonian Theatre was created because it was thought to be improper to conduct university ceremonies in a consecrated building. It was designed by a young Christopher Wren — his first major work — and given by Gilbert Sheldon, Archbishop of Canterbury. Inside, an elaborate ceiling painting shows Truth descending on the Arts and Sciences surrounded by Geometry, Law, Justice, Music, Drama, Architecture and Astronomy.

To the left is the Clarendon Building, built by Nicholas Hawksmoor. It housed the University Press from 1713 to 1829, and is now used by the Bodleian Library.

HAYDN received his honorary degree of Doctor of Music at the Sheldonian Theatre and conducted a symphony since known as the Oxford Symphony.

VEAL RENO

Serves 4

Calvados and cream combine to add a rich finish to this tasty dish from La Cantina — Oxford's original trattoria.

Metric		*lb/oz*	*U.S.A.*
	4 × 6 oz Veal escalopes		
50 g	*Butter*	2 oz	¼ cup
1 tbsp	*Oil*	1 tbsp	1 tbsp
2	*Onions, chopped*	2	2
1	*Red pepper, chopped*	1	1
150 g	*Mushrooms, sliced*	6 oz	1¾ cups
100 g	*Apple purée*	4 oz	½ cup
2 tbsp	*Single cream*	2 tbsp	3 tbsp
2 tbsp	*Calvados*	2 tbsp	2 tbsp

1. Melt half the butter in a saucepan over a gentle heat and add a little oil. Fry the onion gently until transparent. When the onion is cooked add the red pepper and cook for a few minutes.
2. Add the mushrooms and when cooked, stir in the apple purée. Heat through and add salt and pepper to taste.
3. Add the cream but do not let the mixture boil. Keep the sauce warm.
4. In another pan melt the remaining butter and fry the escalopes on both sides until cooked. Pour over the Calvados and flambé.
5. Transfer to a warm serving dish and pour a little of the sauce over the meat. Serve the rest of the sauce separately.

SHELLEY MEMORIAL

The poet Shelley is honoured by University College in the form of this extravagant marble memorial. It depicts him "as he lay washed up on the Italian shore" — a somewhat romanticised Victorian interpretation!

The college did not regard Shelley so sympathetically in his student days, however: the authorities sent him down for publishing a pamphlet called "The Necessity of Atheism".

SWEET AND SOUR PORK *Serves 6*

The Opium Den are proud of serving this dish Cantonese style (not in batter!). Follow their instructions for a delicious result.

Metric		*lb/oz*	*U.S.A.*
750 g	*Belly of pork*	1 ½ lb	1 ½ lb
1 tsp	*Monosodium glutamate*	1 tsp	1 tsp
3 tbsp	*Flour*	3 tbsp	4 tbsp
1	*Egg, beaten*	1	1
	Oil for frying		
	For the sauce:		
1 tbsp	*Vinegar*	1 tbsp	1 tbsp
1 tbsp	*Tomato sauce*	1 tbsp	1 tbsp
1 tsp	*Worcestershire sauce*	1 tsp	1 tsp
1 tbsp	*Sugar*	1 tbsp	1 tbsp
6	*Lemon slices*	6	6
125 g	*Sour plums, stoned (optional)*	4 oz	4 oz
1 tbsp	*Cornflour*	1 tbsp	1 tbsp
4 tbsp	*Pineapple, chopped*	4 tbsp	⅔ cup
½	*Green pepper, chopped*	½	½
1	*Onion, chopped*	1	1

1. Remove the skin from the pork and cut into cubes, making sure you have some lean and fat on each piece.
2. Mix together the monosodium glutamate, half the flour, the beaten egg and a pinch of salt. Coat the pork pieces.
3. Season the remaining flour with salt and pepper then use to coat each piece of meat. Deep fry in oil.
4. To make the sauce, mix together in a saucepan the vinegar, tomato sauce, Worcestershire sauce, sugar and a pinch of salt. Add the lemon slices and sour plums. Cook gently until the plums are soft. Sieve the sauce and return the liquor to the saucepan.
5. Mix the cornflour with a little cold water then stir into the sauce. Bring to the boil and stir until thickened.
6. Add the chopped pineapple, green pepper and onion. Simmer for a few minutes then add the pork pieces. Bring back to the boil and transfer to a warm serving dish. Serve with rice or noodles.

"Look at pork. There's a subject!
If you want a subject, look at pork!" Great Expectations
CHARLES DICKENS, 1812-1870

PEASANTS' POTS

Serves 6

A nice idea for individual pork casseroles from Chef Strivens of Browns Restaurant.

Metric		*lb/oz*	*U.S.A.*
375 g	*Leg of pork, diced*	12 oz	12 oz
1 can	*Tomatoes, diced*	1 can	1 can
75 ml	*Red wine*	⅛ pt	¼ cup
1	*Marjoram, pinch of*	1	1
1	*Thyme, pinch of*	1	1
1 tsp	*Granulated sugar*	1 tsp	1 tsp
2	*Dried chillis, soaked and chopped*	2	2
1	*Large onion, sliced*	1	1
1	*Green pepper, sliced*	1	1
2 tbsp	*Tomato purée*	2 tbsp	2 tbsp
1	*Chicken stock cube*	1	1
30 g	*Flour*	1 oz	2 tbsp
30 g	*Butter*	1 oz	2 tbsp
375 g	*Baked beans, butter beans and flageolet beans, mixed*	12 oz	1½ cups
6	*Liver sausage slices*	6	6
6	*Cheddar cheese slices*	6	6

1. Put the pork into a large pan, cover with tomatoes, red wine, herbs, sugar, chilli and a little salt and pepper. If there is not enough liquid to cover the meat, add a little water. Cook the meat until tender, but firm.
2. Add the onions and green peppers. Cook until tender. Add the tomato purée and stock cube.
3. Mix the flour and butter together well in a small bowl and add small knobs to the meat, stirring well until the flour and butter are all mixed in. Stir until the sauce begins to thicken. Add the beans and bring back to the boil.
4. Remove from the stove. Place the mixture in six separate casseroles, and put a slice of liver sausage and a slice of cheese on each. Place in a hot oven, 180°C, 350°F, Gas Mark 4, for 20-25 minutes until the cheese has melted and begins to turn golden brown.

WHEN DID THE COLD MEAT BECOME HOT STUFF?
When it met the Oxford Sauce!

Oxford sauce: Peel zest from 2 oranges and a lemon. Cut in thin strips, plunge into boiling water for 5 minutes, then strain and set aside. In a heavy pan mix the fruit juice, 8 tbsp redcurrant jelly, 1 tbsp English mustard and 2 tsp ground ginger. Heat and stir continuously till smooth. Stir in 8 tbsp port. Simmer gently for 20 minutes, then season to taste. Store in sterilised jars in a cool place.

CHERWELL CUTLETS *Serves 4*

An unusual recipe for lamb cutlets in a tomato and artichoke sauce from Ladbroke Linton Lodge.

Metric		*lb/oz*	*U.S.A.*
	12 Lamb cutlets		
30 g	*Butter*	1 oz	2 tbsp
30 g	*Onions, chopped*	1 oz	2 tbsp
50 g	*Mushrooms, sliced*	2 oz	¾ cup
4	*Tomatoes, chopped*	4	4
4	*Artichoke bottoms, sliced*	4	4
75 ml	*White wine*	⅛ pt	¼ cup
300 ml	*Demi-glace sauce (see p. 30)*	½ pt	1 cup
3 tbsp	*Oil for frying*	3 tbsp	4 tbsp
3 tbsp	*Parsley, chopped*	3 tbsp	4 tbsp

1. Melt the butter in a saucepan, add the onions and mushrooms, and cook for 1 minute.
2. Add the tomatoes and artichoke bottoms, white wine and demi-glace sauce. Leave to simmer for a few minutes.
3. Heat the oil in a frying pan, season with salt and pepper and fry the lamb cutlets.
4. Lay the cutlets neatly on a serving dish, pour the sauce over and sprinkle with chopped parsley.

LOOK OUT for 83 St Aldate's as this is the shop kept by the sheep with knitting needles in Lewis Carroll's "Through the Looking Glass".

KEBLE COLLEGE

Opened in 1870, Keble stands out among other Oxford colleges for its red brick construction and Victorian Gothic design. It is also unusual for not being built on the "staircase" principle, but has rooms on long corridors. Money was raised by the Reverend John Keble's admirers to found a college for men who could not otherwise afford to come up to Oxford.

Demi-glace sauce

To make a demi-glace sauce, put equal quantities of Espagnole sauce (below) and strong beef stock into a heavy pan (with a few mushrooms if available).

Simmer until the sauce is reduced by at least half. Remove, strain and re-heat. Remove from the heat and stir in a small glassful of dry sherry.

Espagnole sauce

Metric		*lb/oz*	*U.S.A.*
25 g	*Ham or bacon (raw), chopped*	1 tbsp	1 tbsp
25 g	*Butter*	1 oz	1 tbsp
1	*Carrot, peeled and chopped*	1	1
1	*Onion*	1	1
3 tbsp	*Mushroom stalks, chopped*	3 tbsp	4 tbsp
2 tbsp	*Celery, chopped (optional)*	2 tbsp	3 tbsp
1 tsp	*Thyme*	1 tsp	1 tsp
1	*Bay leaf*	1	1
40 g	*Flour*	1 ½ oz	¼ cup
1	*Beef stock cube*	1	1
1 tbsp	*Tomato paste*	2 tbsp	3 tbsp
250 g	*Tomatoes, peeled and chopped*	½ lb	2 cups

ST EDMUND HALL

The only surviving medieval hall in the University, the college, with its pretty quadrangle, is found behind an unprepossessing exterior in Queen's Lane. The classical building on the far side houses the library, which removed chains from its books in 1760.

1. Cook the bacon in the butter for a few minutes.
2. Add the vegetables and sauté gently for 5-8 minutes.
3. Make a stock with the cube and 300 ml (½ pt) boiling water, and set aside.
4. Stir the flour into the vegetable mixture. Continue stirring until the flour browns well, then add the stock very gradually, stirring continuously.
5. When the sauce has thickened, stir in the tomato paste, tomatoes, thyme and bay leaf. Season lightly.
6. Simmer for 30 minutes, stirring occasionally and skimming off excess fat. Taste and correct the seasoning.
7. Strain the sauce into a basin and cover the surface with damp greaseproof paper or clingwrap to prevent a skin forming.

CHICKEN VERONICA

Serves 2

White grapes (being green!) add a bright touch to this creamy chicken dish made aromatic by the addition of tarragon. This recipe comes from La Cantina.

Metric		*lb/oz*	*U.S.A.*
	2 Chicken breasts (supremes)		
50 g	*Butter*	2 oz	¼ cup
1	*Small onion, chopped*	1	1
125 g	*Button mushrooms*	4 oz	1 cup
2 tbsp	*White wine*	2 tbsp	3 tbsp
50 g	*White grapes, peeled and pipped**	2 oz	½ cup
150 ml	*Béchamel sauce (see p. 60)*	¼ pt	½ cup
1	*Tarragon, pinch of*	1	1
2 tbsp	*Single cream*	2 tbsp	2 tbsp

1. Melt the butter in a large pan and fry the supremes until lightly browned.
2. Add the onions and fry until tender. Add the mushrooms and cook for a few minutes.
3. Add the wine and grapes, stir in the béchamel sauce and add the tarragon. Season to taste, stir in the cream and reheat (but do not boil).
4. Transfer the supremes to a warm serving dish and pour over the sauce.

**White seedless grapes may be used whole and unpeeled when in season — Editor.*

LEMON CHICKEN CANTONESE STYLE *Serves 4*

This light and pretty dish from the Opium Den may be served as part of a Chinese meal or with vegetables.

Metric		*lb/oz*	*U.S.A.*
	4 Chicken breasts (supremes)		
4 tbsp	*Flour*	4 tbsp	4 tbsp
1	*Egg, beaten*	1	1
	Oil for frying		
1	*Lemon, squeezed*	1	1
2 tsp	*Sugar*	2 tsp	2 tsp
1	*Egg white*	1	1
4	*Lemon slices*	4	4

1. Slice the supremes into thin slices (5 mm, ¼").
2. Put 3 tbsp of the flour on to a flat plate. Beat the egg in a bowl with ½ tsp of salt.
3. Dip the chicken pieces into the egg, then into the flour and deep fry in oil. Transfer to a warm plate and keep warm.
4. Whisk together in a bowl the lemon juice, sugar, 300 ml (½ pt, 1 cup) hot water and remaining flour, making sure the flour is properly dissolved. Pour into a saucepan and heat until boiling, stirring all the time, until the sauce has thickened. Adjust sweetness to taste.
5. Just before serving, stir in the egg white so that it forms strands. Pour over the chicken and top with lemon slices.

POULET EN POT A LA MARENGO *Serves 8*

Wren's Restaurant specialises in fish dishes. This one is unusual in that crayfish is combined with chicken.

Metric		*lb/oz*	*U.S.A.*
	1 Large chicken or 8 pieces		
50g	*Flour, seasoned*	2 oz	3 tbsp
4 tbsp	*Oil*	4 tbsp	5 tbsp
2	*Shallots or small onions, chopped*	2	2
150 ml	*Chicken stock*	¼ pt	½ cup
300 ml	*Dry white wine*	½ pt	1 cup
250 g	*Mushrooms, quartered*	8 oz	2 cups
4	*Tomatoes, peeled and chopped*	4	4
1 tbsp	*Tomato purée*	1 tbsp	1 tbsp
6	*Live crayfish*	6	6
1 tbsp	*Basil, chopped (fresh if possible — use half quantity if dried)*	1 tbsp	1 tbsp

1. If using a whole chicken, cut into pieces. Wash the chicken pieces and coat in flour seasoned with salt and pepper.

2. Heat the oil in a large pan and add the chicken and shallots. Lightly brown the chicken all over, then add the stock and simmer gently for 15 minutes.
3. Transfer the chicken to an ovenproof casserole and set aside. Add to the pan the wine, mushrooms, tomatoes and tomato purée. Bring to the boil and simmer for 2 or 3 minutes. Season to taste. Pour the sauce over the chicken (setting the pan aside for later use) and place in a preheated oven, 180°C, 350°F, Gas Mark 4, for 25 minutes.
4. Just before serving, strain off some of the liquid into the pan, bring to the boil and add the crayfish and basil. Cook for a few minutes (3 to 6 minutes, according to size) then transfer the crayfish and liquor to the chicken. Serve with boiled rice.

"Undergraduates owe their happiness chiefly to the consciousness that they are no longer at school. The nonsense which was knocked out of them at school is all put gently back at Oxford or Cambridge."

Going Back to School
SIR MAX BEERBOHM, 1872-1956

PETTI DI POLLO REALE

Serves 4

A wonderfully rich creation from Giovanni Ventriglia of the Saraceno Restaurant.

Metric		*lb/oz*	*U.S.A.*
	4 Chicken breasts		
30 g	*Flour, seasoned*	1 oz	2 tbsp
50 g	*Butter*	2 oz	¼ cup
1 tbsp	*Brandy*	1 tbsp	1 tbsp
1	*Onion, chopped*	1	1
125 g	*Mushrooms, chopped*	4 oz	1 cup
150 ml	*White wine*	¼ pt	½ cup
150 ml	*Double cream*	¼ pt	½ cup
	Fresh or canned asparagus for garnish		

1. Cut each chicken breast horizontally into two slices.
2. Coat them in the flour seasoned with salt and pepper.
3. Melt half the butter in a large pan and fry the chicken for a few minutes on each side until tender. Pour over the brandy and flambe'.
4. Remove from the pan and place on a warm serving dish.
5. Put the remaining butter in the pan and gently fry the onions until transparent but not brown.
6. Add the mushrooms and cook for a few minutes.
7. Pour over the white wine and heat through. Stir in the cream and simmer gently until the sauce has thickened.
8. Spoon the sauce over the chicken and garnish with fresh cooked (or heated canned) asparagus.

L'AIGUILLETTES DE CANARD SAUVAGE A L'ARMAGNAC
WILD DUCK BREASTS IN ARMAGNAC *Serves 4*

The kitchens of La Sorbonne are a hive of industry with a team of chefs preparing and creating a range of delicacies under the direction of the flamboyant proprietor and chef de cuisine M. Chavagnon. This busy and very successful restaurateur also runs the adjoining Casse-Croute and Bleu Blanc Rouge restaurants. This recipe is one of his favourites.

Metric		*lb/oz*	*U.S.A.*
	2 Mallards (wild duck)		
50 g	*Granulated sugar*	2 oz	4 tbsp
10 g	*Peppercorns, crushed*	½ oz	1 tbsp
3 tbsp	*Vinegar*	3 tbsp	5 tbsp
4	*Shallots or small onions, chopped*	4	4
1 tbsp	*Tomato purée*	1 tbsp	1 tbsp
2	*Garlic cloves, crushed*	2	2
1	*Bouquet garni*	1	1
500 ml	*Red wine (vintage Burgundy)*	¾ pt	1½ cups
500 ml	*Chicken stock (or bouillon made from 2 chicken stock cubes)*	¾ pt	1½ cups
3 tbsp	*Armagnac*	3 tbsp	5 tbsp
2 tsp	*Arrowroot*	2 tsp	2 tsp
100 g	*Chicken liver pâté*	4 oz	½ cup
1 tbsp	*Redcurrant jelly*	1 tbsp	1 tbsp
100 g	*Butter*	4 oz	½ cup
1 tbsp	*Double cream*	1 tbsp	1 tbsp
4	*Slices of bread for croûtons*	4	4
2 tbsp	*Oil for frying*	2 tbsp	2 tbsp

1. Place the ducks in a very hot oven, 220°C, 425°F, Gas Mark 7 for 10-12 minutes to seal the meat. With a sharp knife, remove the four breasts and skin them. Slice into long aiguillettes and arrange in a preheated buttered casserole, which must be ovenproof and suitable for flambéing.
2. Put the sugar, crushed peppercorns and 1 tbsp water into a deep saucepan. Using a wooden spatula, stir the mixture over a high heat until it turns golden in colour. Add the vinegar and boil until it becomes a syrup.
3. Break up the duck carcasses, reserving the legs for another recipe. Add the crushed carcasses, shallots, tomato purée, garlic, bouquet garni and red wine to the syrup and cook until the liquid has reduced by a quarter.
4. Add the chicken stock and half the Armagnac and boil again to reduce by one quarter. Pass the stock through a sieve and bring to the boil.
5. Mix the arrowroot with a little water and add to the stock until a nice thickness is obtained. Add half the chicken liver

pâté and the redcurrant jelly. Boil for 15 minutes, stirring frequently. Remove from the heat and skim off any fat.

6. Put the casserole into a preheated oven, 190°C, 375°F, Gas Mark 5, for approximately 4 minutes*. Remove from the oven and put one slice of pâté on each aiguillette. Pour over the remainder of the Armagnac and flambé.
7. Bring the sauce back to the boil. Remove from the heat and add the butter and cream, stirring until smooth. Pass through a sieve on to the aiguillettes and top with the fried croûtons.

**Four minutes if you like your duck pink; a little longer if you don't! — Editor.*

ST CECILIA WINDOW

The patron saint of music is depicted in the central panel of this stained-glass window in Christ Church Cathedral. It was designed by Sir Edward Burne-Jones, a former undergraduate of Exeter College.

QUAIL WITH GREEN PEPPERCORNS *Serves 8*

Don't quail! This recipe, from Chef Maguire of the Randolph Hotel, takes the strain out of cooking and serving these delicious little game birds.

Metric		*lb/oz*	*U.S.A.*
	8 Quail		
2 tbsp	*Soft green peppercorns*	2 tbsp	2 tbsp
125 g	*Butter*	4 oz	½ cup
300 ml	*Chicken stock*	½ pt	1 cup
1 tbsp	*Sherry*	1 tbsp	1 tbsp
4 tbsp	*Parsley, chopped*	4 tbsp	6 tbsp

1. Squash half of the peppercorns on to the quail and season.
2. Place half the butter into a large pan and sauté the quail until nicely browned. Drain and place in a casserole. Add the remaining peppercorns, stock and sherry.
3. Place in a hot oven, 190°C, 375°F, Gas Mark 5, for 15 minutes until the quail are tender.
4. Pour off the liquor into a small pan and boil until reduced by half. Remove from heat and whisk in remaining butter.
5. Place the quail on a heated serving dish and pour over the sauce. Garnish with parsley.

QUAIL AND WALNUT SALAD *Serves 4*

This combination of hot game and cool crispy salad is a delicious dish for a small dinner party. The recipe comes from Les Quat' Saisons Restaurant Francais. Try it with poussins if quail are not available.

Metric		*lb/oz*	*U.S.A.*
	4 Quail		
	Winter salad vegetables eg, curly endive, chicory, red lettuce, lambs' lettuce		
1	*French beans, handful*	1	1
100 g	*Belly of pork, smoked*	4 oz	4 oz
1 tbsp	*Goose fat (or lard)*	1 tbsp	1 tbsp
4	*Button mushrooms, sliced*	4	4
8	*Walnuts, shelled*	8	8
2	*Girolles (wild mushrooms), sliced*	2	2
8 tbsp	*Olive oil, best quality*	8 tbsp	8 tbsp
½	*Lemon, squeezed*	½	½
	Croûtons, dried in the oven		
	White wine vinegar for deglazing		

1. Ask your butcher to prepare the quail, reserving the livers.
2. Wash and drain the salads. Blanch the beans for 3-4 minutes in boiling, salted water until cooked but still crispy. Place in very cold water, so that they retain their colour.
3. Remove the rind from the belly of pork and cut the meat into small strips. Blanch in unsalted boiling water for 5 minutes, then drain.
4. Heat the goose fat in a roasting tin and sauté the quail whole, breast down, for 1 minute until golden. Turn them over and place in a hot oven, 220°C, 425°F, Gas Mark 7 for 7 minutes. Take out of the oven and remove the fat.
5. Place the "lardons" (slivers of bacon) in a pan and heat gently for a few minutes. Slice the livers and add to the pan. Divide the quail into legs and breasts and add to the pan. Season and finish cooking.
6. Reserve a few beans, mushrooms and walnuts for decoration and put the remainder in a bowl with the girolles and winter salads. Add the olive oil, lemon juice and pork and mix well. Season to taste. Arrange the salad on a serving dish. Top with the quail and sliced livers, and decorate with the croûtons and reserved garnishes.
7. Deglaze the pan by adding a dash of vinegar. Bring to the boil, stirring with a wooden spoon so that the vinegar and pan residues amalgamate. Allow to cool slightly, then pour over the salad and add two turns of black pepper.

TURL STREET is so called after a revolving or twirling gate that used to be at one end, while BRASENOSE LANE is the only street in Oxford to retain its medieval central gutter.

MOSAIQUE DE POISSONS MARSEILLAISE
MEDITERRANEAN SEAFOOD MEDLEY

A dish from Wren's Restaurant reminiscent of open-air eating in summer climes. Allow 500 g (1 lb of fresh fish, unboned weight, per person. Choose a varied selection from the following: Red mullet, squid or monkfish; mussels, prawns, crab or other shellfish; small bass or whiting. Allow the following vegetables for each person:

Metric		*lb/oz*	*U.S.A.*
	Shallots or small onions, chopped (to taste)		
½	*Garlic clove, crushed*	½	½
	Fennel bulb, chopped (to taste)		
50 g	*Red, yellow and green peppers, sliced*	2 oz	2 oz
50 g	*Courgettes, sliced*	2 oz	2 oz
125 g	*Tomatoes, peeled*	4 oz	4 oz
	Olive oil		
1	*Rind of orange, finely sliced*	1	1
1	*Lemon, juice of*	1	1
1 tbsp	*Parsley, chopped*	1 tbsp	1 tbsp

1. Clean and prepare all fish and vegetables.
2. Stew the squid in seasoned olive oil for 30 minutes.
3. Gently sauté the vegetables in oil starting with the shallots, then add the garlic, fennel, peppers, courgettes and tomatoes. Sprinkle with orange rind and lemon juice and set aside when the vegetables are tender, but not overcooked.
4. Open the mussels* and grill with the red mullet or bass until tender. Arrange the vegetables on a hot dish and place the cooked fish and squid on top. Cover with foil and place in the oven to keep warm. 180°C, 350°F, Gas Mark 4.
5. Meanwhile fry scallops of monkfish in squid cooking oil. When they are golden, but still moist, use to garnish the dish.
6. Pour over the pan juices and sprinkle with chopped parsley. Serve with garlic bread.

*If you find this difficult, cook the mussels in boiling water until they are open. See footnote on mussels on page 42 — Editor.

NEW COLLEGE CARVING *(left)* & BROAD STREET CROSS

Look up and you will be rewarded by the sight of some intricate and often amusing carvings — like this one on the bell-tower of New College. Spot the cross set in the middle of Broad Street, marking where the Protestant martyrs, Cranmer, Latimer and Ridley, were burned at the stake.

COQUILLES ST JACQUES A LA JULIENNE DE LEGUMES
SCALLOPS, QUENELLES & JULIENNE OF VEGETABLES IN VERMOUTH SAUCE

Serves 4

A rich haute cuisine speciality from M. Blanc of Les Quat' Saisons Restaurant Francais.

Metric		*lb/oz*	*U.S.A.*
26	*Scallops*	26	26
2	*Celery sticks*	2	2
2	*Carrots*	2	2
2	*Leeks*	2	2
250 g	*Fillet of brill*	8 oz	8 oz
1	*Egg, separated*	1	1
225 ml	*Double cream*	7 fl oz	¾ cup
12	*Button mushrooms*	12	12
100 ml	*Noilly Prat*	3½ fl oz	⅓ cup
100 ml	*Fish stock (made with fish trimmings and bones — ask fishmonger!)*	3½ fl oz	⅓ cup
150 ml	*Whipping cream*	4 fl oz	½ cup
30 g	*Butter*	1 oz	2 tbsp
½	*Lemon, squeezed*	½	½
	Fleurons to decorate (see p. 18)		

1. Open the scallops over a fine strainer and bowl to catch the juice, sliding a knife close against the flat shell and cutting the muscle. Remove the meat and coral, discard the membranes but keep the juice. Wash the scallops in plenty of water, cut them in two and set aside.
2. Cut the celery, carrots and white of leeks into fine julienne strips. Simmer the celery and carrots in a little water, to a crisp texture, but leave the leeks raw.
3. To make the quenelles, liquidise the brill with 6 of the scallops. Refrigerate for an hour.
4. Return to the blender and add ½ tsp salt. Gradually add the egg white and double cream, season to taste, and refrigerate for another hour.
5. Put the scallops, leeks, carrots, celery and mushrooms in a steamer, and steam for 2 minutes.
6. Meanwhile, reduce the Noilly Prat to 1 tbsp, add the fish stock, the natural and cooking juices of the scallops and reduce to about one third. Whip 1 tbsp of the whipping cream and set aside. Add the remainder to the fish stock and bring to the boil.
7. Remove from the heat and bind with the egg yolk. Work in the butter and add the whipped cream. Season to taste and add the lemon juice.
8. Shape the quenelles with two spoons dipped in hot water, then poach them in salted water for 4 minutes at simmering point.
9. To serve, place the scallops, quenelles and vegetables on four warmed plates, coat them with the sauce and glaze

under a grill until light golden in colour. Decorate with pastry fleurons.

BAKED SEA BASS WITH CORIANDER *Serves 4*

An aromatic fish dish cooked in lemon and white wine, from the Randolph Hotel.

Metric		*lb/oz*	*U.S.A.*
	4 × 175 g (6 oz) Sea bass steaks		
50 g	*Butter, melted*	2 oz	¼ cup
2 tsp	*Coriander, ground*	2 tsp	2 tsp
2	*Lemons*	2	2
½ bott	*White wine*	½ bott	½ bott
3 tbsp	*Parsley*	3 tbsp	4 tbsp

1. Cover the bottom of a lidded casserole dish with the butter.
2. Rub the steaks with the coriander and season with salt. Arrange in the dish.
3. Squeeze the juice from one lemon over the fish and add the wine.
4. Bake the fish in a preheated oven, 190°C, 375°F, Gas Mark 5, for 15 minutes.
5. When cooked, garnish with the parsley and the remaining lemon, cut into wedges.

STUDENTS RETURNING to their college after gates are locked might think twice before attempting to use this drainpipe as a means of entry!

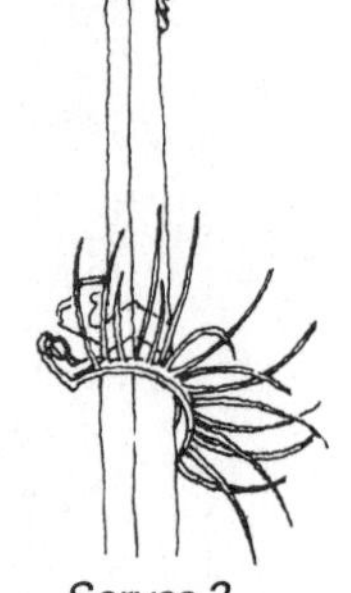

CHARLES I'S ARTILLERY was stationed in University Park (known as the Parks) in 1642. In the south-east corner is Parson's Pleasure, famous for its tradition of nude bathing, where women have to leave their punts and walk discreetly round the bathing area!

TROUT ISIS *Serves 2*

The Isis Hotel's simple but delicious recipe for trout, which are now readily available fresh and frozen.

Metric		*lb/oz*	*U.S.A.*
	2 trout		
4	*Back bacon rashers*	4	4
	Bacon fat for frying		

1. Split the trout up the belly, leaving the two halves attached by the skin at the back. Remove the back bone and place a rasher of bacon over the flesh of each half.
2. Fry gently in bacon fat on both sides until the fish is cooked through and the skin and the bacon are just brown.
3. Serve with the bacon still in place.

THE HIGH STREET

"The High" is dominated by the thirteenth century spire of St Mary the Virgin, the University church; next to it is All Souls and in the foreground, Queen's College. The tree is remarkable — and famous — for being the only one in the High Street.

EASTGATE HOTEL, further down the High Street, marks the site of the old East gate of the city, removed in 1771, while St Michael-at-the-North-Gate was part of the city wall defences. The church's tower is built from "random rubble" and is the oldest building in the city — early eleventh century.

RICE IN PAELLA

Serves 6

Senor Lopez of the Elizabeth Restaurant points out that *paella* is the name of a large flat cooking dish and not the meal most usually associated with it. Either way, his recipe is undoubtedly authentic, not difficult, and sure to create an impression when served.

Metric		*lb/oz*	*U.S.A.*
250 g	*Chicken flesh*	8 oz	8 oz
12	*Mussels*	12	12
250 g	*Scampi*	8 oz	8 oz
3 tbsp	*Olive oil*	3 tbsp	3 tbsp
1	*Garlic clove, finely chopped*	1	1
3	*Tomatoes, peeled and chopped*	3	3
1	*Small green pepper, chopped*	1	1
1	*Small red pepper, chopped*	1	1
250 g	*Long grain rice*	8 oz	8 oz
1 litre	*Chicken stock*	1½ pt	3 cups
1	*Saffron, pinch of*	1	1

1. Put half the oil in a large flameproof casserole or paella and when hot, brown the chicken, turning occasionally. Remove the chicken from the pan and keep warm.
2. Scrub and clean the mussels* then add to the pan with the scampi. Cook for a few minutes until the mussels open. With a strainer spoon, remove the mussels and scampi and keep warm.
3. Add a little more oil to the pan and add the chicken, garlic, tomatoes and peppers. Cook gently until the chicken is tender.
4. Add rice and stir well. Pour in stock and season. Stir in the saffron and cook gently for 15 minutes.
5. Return seafood to pan and cook for 5 minutes. Remove from heat and leave paella to rest for 5 minutes. Do not stir until serving.

**Do not use any with broken shells and discard any which do not open after cooking — Editor.*

MARTYRS' MEMORIAL

Sir Gilbert Scott's memorial commemorates the 1555 "Oxford Martyrs" — Cranmer, Latimer and Ridley, Protestants who were executed in Mary Tudor's reign. All Cambridge men, they were tried at the University Church, also the scene of sermons by Wesley, Keble and Newman, the latter starting the Oxford Movement which set out to revitalise the Church of England.

ALL SOULS Built to commemorate Henry V's victorious battles, All Souls was so named because it was established for the saying of masses for the souls of those who died in the French wars. To this day it admits only graduates — a policy dating from medieval times.

BALLIOL This college was founded by John de Bailleul in the thirteenth century as part of a penance which he had to pay to the Bishop of Durham. John de Bailleul was responsible for the maintenance of sixteen poor scholars; his widow, Dervorguilla, continued this work after his death and issued a charter in 1282 which is still in the possession of the college.

BRASENOSE The college takes its name from the brazen nosed door knocker of the original medieval hall which used to occupy the site. It is now displayed above the High Table.

CHRIST CHURCH Officially "The House of Christ's Cathedral in Oxford", but known as "The House", this is the largest college in Oxford. Endowed by Henry VIII, it was founded by Cardinal Wolsey, whose hat is displayed in the library.

CORPUS CHRISTI When founded in the sixteenth century, the college provided for twenty *discipuli*, aged between 12 and 17. When other colleges surrendered their gold and silver to Charles I in 1642, Corpus somehow managed to keep its treasures, including gold communion vessels and the staff of the founder (Richard Fox, Bishop of Exeter, Bath and Wells, Durham and Winchester successively!).

EXETER Founded by the Bishop of Exeter in 1314, this college still has West Country connections, and boasts a hall built in 1618.

HERTFORD Originally Hart Hall, founded in the thirteenth century by Elias de Hertford the present college was refounded in 1874 through the benefaction of banker, Thomas Baring. Most of the buildings are comparatively modern, but the library is eighteenth century.

JESUS This was the only college to be founded in Elizabeth I's reign. It has a strong Welsh connection, and the new quadrangle was opened by the Prince of Wales in 1971.

KEBLE Built by public subscription as a memorial to the Rev John Keble, it was intended to combine a university education with principles of the Church of England.

LADY MARGARET HALL Begun in 1878 in a private house with nine women students, this college is called after Henry VII's mother, Lady Margaret Beaufort, who founded Christ's and St John's colleges at Cambridge.

LINACRE Founded in 1962 for postgraduates, this college was named after Thomas Linacre, great Renaissance scholar and physician who founded the London College of Physicians.

LINCOLN Dr John Radcliffe (who left money to build the Camera) was a Fellow in the seventeenth century as also was John Wesley in 1726. The college owns the Mitre Hotel, a lovely old building which has accommodated undergraduates since 1968.

MAGDALEN (pronounced Maudlin) was the wealthiest foundation in the university when founded in 1458 by William of Waynflete who incorporated part of the Hospital of St John's into the college. Students needed knowledge of plainsong and grammar and had to speak Latin. The college was the first to allocate rooms for high-born youths, who wore braided silk gowns and were known as "gentlemen commoners".

MANSFIELD Founded as a theological college in the nineteenth century for the Congregational Church, it still trains students for the ministry, but most undergraduates read other subjects.

MERTON Founded in 1264, this is the oldest college in Oxford. Its library, dating back to 1370, is the oldest in England. The college contains the only completely stone room in Oxford, the muniments room, in which college records are kept. Both Merton and New College claim the distinction of having established the tradition of college quadrangles.

NEW William of Wykeham, who lived in the fourteenth century, was a very busy man — he not only founded New College, but was also responsible for the rebuilding of Winchester Cathedral and the founding of Winchester School! Members never had to take a test for their degrees — they were simply pronounced fit by the Warden — this practice was not revoked until 1834.

NUFFIELD Founded by Sir William Morris, Viscount Nuffield, the college aims to have Fellows who can give researchers the benefit of their practical experience. They have included captains of industry and trade union leaders. The college motto (Let justice be done) may seem an ironic one for the founder — in Latin it is *Fiat justitia*!

ORIEL A college which probably takes its name from an original building with an oriel window (a bay window on an upper storey).

PEMBROKE Nominally founded by King James I, its southern boundary is the old city wall. The Master's Lodgings were formerly Cardinal Wolsey's almshouses, and the college's latest building was named after its Chancellor, Harold Macmillan, in 1977.

QUEEN'S The statutes provided that courses in Theology should last 18 years, that Fellows should wear red gowns to commemorate Christ's death, and that they should be summoned to dinner by a trumpet. Today only the last is observed.

RUSKIN To enable working men without the usual entrance requirements to study at the University, two Americans founded this college at the turn of the century. After taking a diploma, many members go on to another college to read for a degree.

ST ANNE'S One of the early women's colleges, it was founded in the nineteenth century with the cosy title of "The Society of Oxford Home Students".

ST ANTONY'S Opened in 1950 on the site of a convent, with money provided by a French merchant, the college offers post-graduate courses in politics, economics and modern history.

ST CATHERINE'S Founded in the nineteenth century for poor students not belonging to a college, St Catherine's is now housed in modern buildings. It is unusual in having only one architect — a Dane, Arne Jacobsen — and in not having a chapel.

ST CROSS The temporary home of this college, founded in 1965, is in part of the old St Cross parish school.

ST EDMUND HALL The only medieval hall to survive in Oxford, the college was named after Sir Edmund of Abingdon who was a tutor at the University before becoming Archbishop of Canterbury.

ST HILDA'S A women's college founded by the Principal of Cheltenham Ladies College, St Hilda's opened its doors in 1893.

ST HUGH'S This women's college was founded in the nineteenth century by Elizabeth Wordsworth (then Principal of Lady Margaret Hall), great-niece of the poet. Its first undergraduates were poorer students who could not afford the fees at Lady Margaret Hall.

ST JOHN'S Dedicated in 1555 to St John the Baptist, the patron saint of tailors, by Sir Thomas White who was a wealthy merchant tailor, the college still has close links with Merchant Taylors' School.

ST PETER'S Founded in 1928, the college occupies the site of New Inn Hall, where Charles I set up a mint for turning college plate into money during the Civil War. One Principal of New Inn Hall was the University's first Member of Parliament.

SOMERVILLE Probably one of the most famous women's colleges, it was named after mathematician Mary Somerville, 1780-1872, and began with twelve students in a private house in 1879.

TRINITY Established to replace Durham College, a Benedictine establishment suppressed at the dissolution, Trinity has successfully absorbed a variety of buildings dating from the thirteenth century onwards.

UNIVERSITY Although its statutes are sixteen years later than Merton's, University College used to take precedence over Merton and Balliol in the University Calendar because it was widely believed to have been founded by Alfred the Great. Its chapel windows depict famous Bible stories.

WADHAM The buildings of Wadham remain much as they were 350 years ago when the college was founded by Nicholas and Dorothy Wadham.

WOLFSON Students, all postgraduates, are housed in modern buildings next to the River Cherwell. Founded in 1966 with money given by the Wolfson and Ford Foundations, the residential accommodation is unusual in that flats are provided for both single people and families.

WORCESTER According to the Edwardian writer Sir Lawrence Jones, the college was popularly known as "Wuggins". One ancient custom still continued today is the waking of undergraduates by hammering a wooden mallet on the door of each staircase.

OXFORD UNIVERSITY PRESS prints several million Bibles a year. Its first book was probably printed in 1478, soon after Caxton printed his first book at Westminster.

BANANA CHEESECAKE *Serves 6*

Honey, bananas and a dash of rose-water combine to give an unusual flavour to this cheesecake served at Browns Restaurant.

Metric		*lb/oz*	*U.S.A.*
250 g	*Digestive biscuits*	8 oz	8 oz
125 g	*Butter*	4 oz	½ cup
1 tbsp	*Golden syrup*	1 tbsp	1 tbsp
300 ml	*Double cream*	½ pt	1 cup
375 g	*Curd cheese*	12 oz	12 oz
1 tbsp	*Honey*	1 tbsp	1 tbsp
50 g	*Caster sugar*	2 oz	4 tbsp
1	*Rose-water, dash of*	1	1
3	*Bananas, chopped*	3	3
2	*Lemons, juice of*	2	2
1 pkt	*Gelatine*	1 pkt	1 pkt

1. To make the base of the cheesecake, crush the biscuits with a rolling pin or in a liquidiser. Reserve some biscuit crumbs for decoration.
2. Melt the butter and golden syrup together and stir into the biscuits.
3. Press the mixture into a 20 cm (8") flan tin. Place in the refrigerator to set.
4. Place the cream in a bowl and whip lightly.
5. Stir in the curd cheese, honey, sugar, rose-water and a pinch of salt.
6. Liquidise the bananas with the lemon juice. Stir into the mixture, then beat together well.
7. Dissolve the gelatine in 15 ml (1 tbsp) warm water and add to the mixture.
8. Pour into the base. Level and sprinkle around the edge with biscuit crumbs. Place in the refrigerator until set.

CHARLOTTE AUX FRAISES

Serves 4

A delicate June speciality from Maison Blanc Patisserie Francaise.

Metric		*lb/oz*	*U.S.A.*
350 g	*Strawberries*	¾ lb	3 cups
3	*Gelatine leaves**	3	3
150 g	*Icing sugar*	5 oz	⅔ cup
½	*Lemon, squeezed*	½	½
4	*Egg whites*	4	4
250 ml	*Double cream*	½ pt	1 cup
1 pkt	*Boudoir biscuits (sponge fingers)*	1 pkt	1 pkt
1 tbsp	*Strawberry jam*	1 tbsp	1 tbsp

1. Soak the gelatine in a little cold water until soft, then drain.
2. Reserve a third of the berries for decoration, and mash the remainder to a pulp with a fork.
3. Warm the pulp gently, remove from the heat and stir in the gelatine and 50 g (2 oz, 4 tbsp) of the icing sugar. Add the lemon juice and set aside. Whip the cream.
4. Whip the egg whites until stiff, add the remaining icing sugar and whisk again until stiff. Add to the strawberry mixture, then add the whipped cream.
5. Line the sides and bottom of a charlotte mould with boudoir biscuits. Pour in the strawberry mousse and leave in a cool place to set.
6. Turn the charlotte out of the mould. Cut the remaining strawberries in two to decorate the top. Sieve and heat the jam, with a little water added, to boiling point. Allow to cool a little then pour over the top of the charlotte to glaze.

**Or 1 packet — Editor.*

ZABAGLIONE AL MARSALA

Serves 4

Learn how to make this classic Italian sweet by following these instructions from the chef of the Saraceno Restaurant.

Metric		*lb/oz*	*U.S.A.*
	4 Egg yolks		
4 tbsp	*Caster sugar*	4 tbsp	5 tbsp
4 tbsp	*Marsala wine*	4 tbsp	5 tbsp

1. Place the egg yolks and the sugar in a mixing bowl over a pan of hot water and beat until the mixture becomes thick and creamy.
2. Add the Marsala and continue beating until the mixture begins to thicken again.
3. Remove from the heat and pour into individual serving dishes.

OLD-FASHIONED FRUIT PUDDING *Serves 8*

A lightly spiced fruit and nut dessert served with brandy balls. This recipe comes from Jane Lodge of the Isis Hotel.

Metric		*lb/oz*	*U.S.A.*
250 g	*Butter*	8 oz	1 cup
250 g	*Soft light brown sugar*	8 oz	1 cup
90 g	*Raisins, seedless*	3 oz	¾ cup
30 g	*Walnuts, chopped*	1 oz	¼ cup
2	*Bananas, finely chopped*	2	2
2	*Dessert apples, peeled and finely chopped*	2	2
2	*Oranges, rind of*	2	2
2	*Eggs*	2	2
275 g	*Self-raising flour*	9 oz	1 ¼ cups
2 tsp	*Cinnamon*	2 tsp	2 tsp
150 ml	*Orange juice*	¼ pt	½ cup
	Milk for thinning		
	For the brandy butter balls:		
150 g	*Butter*	6 oz	1 cup
150 g	*Caster sugar*	6 oz	¾ cup
100 ml	*Brandy*	¼ pt	½ cup

1. Melt 75 g (3 oz, ⅓ cup) of the butter in a saucepan over a gentle heat, remove from the heat and stir in 75 g (3 oz, ⅓ cup) of the sugar with the raisins and walnuts. Stir the bananas and apples into the pan.
2. In a bowl, beat the remaining butter and sugar until soft. Grate the rind of the oranges and add to the mixture. Beat in the eggs gradually.
3. Stir in the flour with the cinnamon, and fold into the creamed ingredients with the strained orange juice. Add a little milk if necessary to give a soft dropping consistency.
4. Grease a 2 litre (3 pint, 6 cup) fluted mould and spoon one third of the apple mixture into the base. Spread the cake mixture over the top; repeat the layering twice more, topping with the cake mixture.
5. Bake at 180°C, 350°F, Gas Mark 4 for just over 1 hour, covering with foil towards the end of cooking if the top is already browned.
6. To prepare the brandy butter balls, cream the butter and sugar together, then beat in the brandy a few drops at a time. Roll into balls and refrigerate to harden.
7. Cool the cake in the tin for 15 minutes. Turn it out and serve warm, topped with brandy butter balls.

SPORTING THE OAK Students' rooms often have an inner and an outer door: the outer one left open indicates that the occupant is "at home"; both shut — traditionally known as "sporting the oak" — means the student is out or does not wish to be disturbed.

"BRIDGE OF SIGHS", HERTFORD COLLEGE

The Venetian bridge joins the older part of Hertford College on the right to the North Quad on the left. It crosses New College Lane.

BLACKWELL'S BOOKSHOP

Known to every undergraduate, some of whose parents are rash enough to open accounts here for their offspring, Blackwell's family business has been supplying books to members of the University for generations.

LINTON LODGE SYLLABUB

Serves 4

The seemingly unlikely combination of red wine and light ale with cream produces a rich and delicious creamy dessert.

Metric		*lb/oz*	*U.S.A.*
300 ml	*Double cream*	½ pt	1 cup
150 ml	*Red wine*	¼ pt	½ cup
75 ml	*Light ale*	⅛ pt	¼ cup
50 g	*Caster sugar*	2 oz	4 tbsp
1 tbsp	*Nutmeg, grated*	1 tbsp	1 tbsp

1. Whip the cream until softly thick. Whisk together the cream, red wine, light ale and caster sugar until thick.
2. Spoon into a piping bag and pipe into 4 glass dishes.
3. Place in the refrigerator and chill for 1 hour.
4. Sprinkle with nutmeg and serve topped with a biscuit.

PROFITEROLES WITH HONEY ICE AND TOFFEE SAUCE

Serves 4

A wickedly rich and delicious dessert from the kitchens of Wren's Restaurant.

Choux Pastry

Metric		*lb/oz*	*U.S.A.*
50 g	*Butter*	2 oz	¼ cup
60 g	*Plain flour*	2½ oz	½ cup
2	*Eggs*	2	2

1. Heat the butter with 150 ml (¼ pt, ½ cup) water on a low heat until melted. Pour the sifted flour and a pinch of salt quickly into the butter and water. Remove from the heat and stir vigorously until smooth. Set aside to cool slightly.
2. Beat the eggs lightly and add them to the paste a little at a time. The paste should become a smooth and shiny ball.
3. Pipe small balls of paste on to a damp baking sheet. Place in the centre of a preheated oven, at 200°C, 400°F, Gas Mark 6. After ten minutes turn up to 220°C, 425°F, Gas Mark 7, for about 15 minutes until the profiteroles are light, crisp and golden in colour. Transfer to a cooling rack and pierce the side of each profiterole with a skewer.
4. Just before serving, cut the top off the profiteroles and with a small spoon fill with hard ice-cream. Arrange a plate and pour sauce over. Serve immediately.

Honey ice-cream

Metric		*lb/oz*	*U.S.A.*
2	*Egg yolks*	2	2
150 ml	*Double cream*	¼ pt	½ cup
300 ml	*Milk*	½ pt	1 cup
135 g	*Runny honey*	4½ oz	6 tbsp

1. Whisk the egg yolks and cream.
2. Boil the milk, add the honey and whisk. Bring back to the boil and stir in the egg mixture. Strain through a fine sieve.
3. Place the mixture in an ice-cream making machine for 25-30 minutes or simply firm the ice-cream mixture in the coldest part of a freezer, using a metal container, removing to whisk every ten minutes as it solidifies.

Toffee sauce

Metric		*lb/oz*	*U.S.A.*
250 g	*Granulated sugar*	8 oz	1 cup

1. Put the sugar and 450 ml (¾ pt, 1 ½ cups) of cold water on to a low heat. Stir, and when the sugar is dissolved increase the heat until the mixture is boiling rapidly.
2. When a dark caramel has formed take the saucepan off the heat and add 150 ml (¼ pt, ½ cup) of hot water.
3. Return to the heat and boil until the caramel has thick consistency. Allow to cool.

UPSIDE DOWN PEAR PUDDING *Serves 6*

Any fruit in season may be used in this Turf Tavern recipe.

Metric		*lb/oz*	*U.S.A.*
500 g	*Fruit in season, pears, blackcurrants, rhubarb etc.*	1 lb	1 lb
30 g	*Margarine*	1 oz	2 tbsp
4 tbsp	*Golden syrup*	4 tbsp	6 tbsp
1 tsp	*Ground nutmeg*	1 tsp	1 tsp
125 g	*Butter*	4 oz	½ cup
125 g	*Caster sugar*	4 oz	½ cup
2	*Eggs*	2	2
125 g	*Flour*	4 oz	¾ cup

1. Grease a deep, round cake tin with the margarine and pour in the golden syrup. Sprinkle over the ground nutmeg.
2. Wash the fruit, peel and halve the pears, top and tail the blackcurrants or chop the rhubarb and arrange in the dish.
3. Beat together the butter and sugar until light and fluffy. Add the eggs, beating in a little flour between each egg. Fold in the rest of the flour.
4. Spoon the sponge mixture over the fruit and bake in a moderate oven, 180°C, 350°F, Gas Mark 4 for 25 minutes until the sponge is cooked.
5. Turn out upside down and serve hot with custard or cream.

MERTON STREET

Cyclists are in for a bumpy ride along this pretty street, which is one of few to retain its original cobbles. Behind the houses opposite Merton College is a Royal Tennis court. The Tudor game, bearing little resemblance to the one played at Wimbledon, has been played in Oxford since 1450.

CHILLED ALMOND SOUFFLE *Serves 6*

A crunch 'n' cream combination from the Randolph Hotel.

Metric		*lb/oz*	*U.S.A.*
4	*Eggs*	4	4
50 g	*Caster sugar*	2 oz	4 tbsp
125 g	*Ground almonds*	4 oz	1 cup
5	*Gelatine leaves (or 1 pkt)*	5	5
300 ml	*Double cream*	½ pt	1 cup
50 g	*Browned nibbed (chopped) almonds*	2 oz	½ cup
150 ml	*Whipping cream*	¼ pt	½ cup

1. Separate the eggs. Beat the egg yolks with the sugar and stir in the ground almonds.
2. Soak the gelatine in a little cold water.
3. Place the egg whites in a clean, dry bowl and whisk until stiff. Whip the double cream until stiff and fold into the egg whites.
4. Dissolve the gelatine in a little hot water and add to the yolks. Fold the yolk and almond mixture into the whites and cream thoroughly.
5. Pour the mixture into individual ramekin dishes and chill. Decorate with whipped cream and almonds.

MERTON LOSES ITS PEACOCKS Not in this case, beautiful young men, but the feathered variety! The college had to dispose of them to keep the peace with local residents because the birds responded every time a car sounded its horn on turning the sharp corner of Merton Street.

PRUNE AND PORT MERINGUE PIE

Serves 6

A deliciously alcoholic fruit dessert from Wren's Restaurant.

Metric		*lb/oz*	*U.S.A.*
250 g	*Sweet short crust pastry*	8 oz	8 oz
500 g*	*Prunes, dried or canned*	1 lb*	1 lb*
150 ml	*Port*	¼ pt	½ cup
2	*Eggs*	2	2
125 g	*Double cream*	4 oz	½ cup
3	*Egg whites*	3	3
150 g	*Sugar*	5 oz	½ cup

1. Line a greased flan case with the sweet pastry.
2. If using dried prunes soak them in port and cook; if tinned, strain and soak in port. Fill base with stoned prunes.
3. Whisk together the two eggs and the cream. Pour over the prunes and bake in a hot oven, 200°C, 400°F, Gas Mark 6, until the pastry is cooked and the egg mixture is set.
4. Whisk the egg whites, add half the sugar and continue to beat until stiff. Fold in the remaining sugar.
5. Evenly cover the flan with the meringue and place in a medium oven, 180°C, 350°F, Gas Mark 4, until the meringue is set. Remove from the oven and serve cold.

**Weight after soaking — Editor.*

SAMUEL JOHNSON, undergraduate at Pembroke, was said to drink three bottles of port at a sitting and feel none the worse for it.

GATEAU CITRON

Serves 6

A light-as-air confection from Maison Blanc Patisserie.

Metric		*lb/oz*	*U.S.A.*
125 g	*Caster sugar*	4 oz	½ cup
100 g	*Double cream*	6 tbsp	¼ cup
1	*Lemon, grated rind and juice*	1	1
150 g	*Flour*	5 oz	1 cup
1 tbsp	*Baking powder*	1 tbsp	1 tbsp
2	*Eggs, separated*	2	2
2 tbsp	*Icing sugar*	2 tbsp	3 tbsp

1. Mix together thoroughly the sugar, cream and lemon rind.
2. Add the flour and baking powder and mix well, then stir in the egg yolks.
3. Whisk the egg whites until stiff and fold into the mixture. Transfer to an 18 cm (7″) greased and floured sponge tin.
4. Bake at 180°C, 350°F, Gas Mark 4 for 35 minutes. When the cake is removed from the oven, mix the lemon juice with the icing sugar and pour over the top. Leave until cold before removing from the tin.

TURF'S SPECIAL DESSERT *Serves 6*

This unusual jam and curd tart is a popular pudding at the Turf Tavern, an old inn much frequented by the student population.

Metric		*lb/oz*	*U.S.A.*
250 g	*Shortcrust pastry*	8 oz	8 oz
3 tbsp	*Raspberry jam*	3 tbsp	4 tbsp
3 tbsp	*Lemon curd*	3 tbsp	4 tbsp
125 g	*Ground almonds*	4 oz	1 cup
125 g	*Cooked flaky or puff pastry**	4 oz	4 oz

1. Line a greased 20 cm (8") flan tin with shortcrust pastry.
2. Mix together the jam and the lemon curd and spread over the bottom of the flan.
3. Sprinkle over the ground almonds.
4. Cover with cooked, crumbled flaky pastry and bake in a moderate oven, 180°C, 350°F, Gas Mark 4, for 25-30 minutes.

**This ingredient may not be readily available for the home cook. Lightly crushed cornflakes give a comparable result — Editor.*

"The rule is, jam to-morrow and jam yesterday — but never jam today."
Through the Looking Glass
LEWIS CARROLL, 1832-1898

BANANA CRISPS *Serves 4*

This banana and toffee combination, Kerepek Pisang, makes a sweet and crunchy end to a meal. It is from Munchy Munchy.

Metric		*lb/oz*	*U.S.A.*
	4 Bananas, very firm		
	Oil for frying		
500 g	*Sugar*	1 lb	2 cups
2	*Cinnamon sticks*	2	2
¼ tsp	*Cinnamon, ground*	¼ tsp	¼ tsp

1. Slice the bananas thinly.
2. Heat the oil on a high flame. Deep fry the banana slices until they are golden and crisp. Drain on kitchen paper.
3. Put the sugar in a heavy saucepan with 300 ml (½ pt, 1 cup) of water, add the cinnamon sticks. Heat on a high heat, stirring all the time, until the sugar has dissolved. Bring to the boil. Take care as the mixture can "spit".
4. Add the banana crisps. Stir until well covered. Remove from the heat. Discard the cinnamon sticks.
5. Sprinkle the cinnamon powder all over the banana crisps.
6. Cool well and when cold store in an airtight container.

"When the High Lama asked him whether Shangri-la was not unique in his experience, and if the Western world could offer anything in the least like it, he answered with a smile: 'Well, yes — to be quite frank, it reminds me very slightly of Oxford'."

Lost Horizon
JAMES HILTON, 1900-1954

CANTERBURY QUADRANGLE, ST JOHN'S COLLEGE

Archbishop Laud, Chancellor of the University, built the beautiful Renaissance quadrangle of St John's in 1631-6 for £5,500! He gave King Charles I a lavish banquet in the library, but his generous hospitality did not unfortunately help him ten years later when he was beheaded for his insistence on strict observance of the Prayer Book.

OMELETTE NORMANDE
FRENCH APPLE OMELETTE

Serves 2

A great dessert idea for that unexpected guest given to us by Wren's Restaurant.

Metric		*lb/oz*	*U.S.A.*
	4 Dessert apples		
30 g	*Butter*	1 oz	2 tbsp
2 tbsp	*Caster sugar*	2 tbsp	3 tbsp
2 tbsp	*Calvados*	2 tbsp	3 tbsp
5	*Eggs*	5	5
2 tbsp	*Cream*	2 tbsp	2 tbsp
1 tbsp	*Icing sugar, sifted*	1 tbsp	1 tbsp

1. Peel and core the apples. Slice thinly lengthways. Melt the butter in a non-stick omelette pan and then sauté the apples gently for 3-4 minutes. Reduce the heat, sweeten the apples to taste, and add the Calvados. Remove from the heat and put cooked apples in a warm bowl.
2. Whisk the eggs with the cream and add a little sugar.
3. Pour the egg mixture into the non-stick pan and whisk quickly for 1-2 minutes over a gentle heat.
4. As the egg begins to set, spoon the apples and their liquor on to one half of the omelette. Fold the other half over the apples and turn out of the pan on to the heated plate. Sprinkle with icing sugar and a dash of Calvados and grill for up to 2 minutes. Serve with fresh cream.

BANANA BREAD

Makes a 2 lb loaf

A popular afternoon tea delicacy from the Nosebag Restaurant in St Michael's Street.

Metric		*lb/oz*	*U.S.A.*
50 g	*Butter*	2 oz	¼ cup
50 g	*Lard*	2 oz	¼ cup
175 g	*Caster sugar*	6 oz	¾ cup
2	*Eggs, beaten*	2	2
250 g	*Self-raising flour*	8 oz	2 cups
500 g	*Bananas, mashed*	1 lb	1 lb

1. Cream the butter and lard with the sugar until light and fluffy. Add the eggs, a little at a time.
2. Sift and fold in the flour then add the mashed bananas.
3. Grease a 1 kg (2 lb) loaf tin and line with greased greaseproof paper. Spoon in the mixture and level it off. Bake on the centre shelf of the oven at 170°C, 325°F, Gas Mark 3 for about 1 hour.
4. Check with a skewer: sink it into the bread and if it comes out clean, the bread is cooked. Remove from the oven and cool before turning out of tin. Serve sliced and buttered.

Index

CORPUS CHRISTI SUNDIAL

In the centre of Corpus's front quadrangle is this sixteenth century sundial, surmounted by a pelican, the College's symbol. A perpetual calendar on its pillar was added later.

DESSERTS AND TEATIME TREATS

SAUCES

SAUCES

All sauces used in the recipes in this book appear in the text (see list above), with the exception of Béchamel sauce.

Béchamel sauce

Metric		*lb/oz*	*U.S.A.*
150 ml	*Milk*	¼ pt	⅔ cup
1	*Small onion, chopped*	1	1
1	*Small carrot, chopped*	1	1
1	*Stick of celery, chopped*	1	1
1	*Bay leaf*	1	1
1	*Clove*	1	1
¼ tsp	*Mace, ground*	¼ tsp	¼ tsp
1	*Peppercorn*	1	1
10 g	*Butter*	½ oz	1 tbsp
15 g	*Flour*	¾ oz	1 ½ tbsp

1. Place the milk and vegetables in a saucepan and bring slowly to the boil, then add the herbs and spices. Cover the pan with a tightly fitting lid.
2. Remove the saucepan from the heat and leave covered for half an hour to infuse.
3. Strain off the milk and remove the vegetables from the pan.
4. Melt the butter in the pan slowly, add the flour and cook for a few minutes, stirring all the time. Be careful not to brown the mixture.
5. Stir the flavoured milk gradually into the flour until the mixture is smooth.
6. Bring the sauce to the boil, stirring all the time.

MEASURES & CONVERSIONS

Ingredients are given in metric, Imperial and American measures. **Use measures from one column only**. Teaspoon and tablespoon measures in the metric column correspond to 5 ml and 15 ml respectively.

The table below will help our American readers.

English	American
Baking powder	Baking soda
Caster sugar	Fine granulated sugar
Courgettes	Zucchini
Demerara sugar	Soft, light brown sugar
Digestive biscuits	Graham crackers
Double cream	Heavy cream
Flaked almonds	Slivered almonds
Golden syrup	Light corn syrup
Grill	Broil
Icing sugar	Confectioners' sugar
Lard	White fat
Lemon curd	Lemon cheese
Single cream	Light cream
Spring onions	Scallions
Streaky bacon rashers	Canadian bacon strips
Sultanas	Light raisins

WHEN DID THE SAUSAGE LOSE ITS SKIN?
When it went to Oxford!
Oxford sausages are an old English dish. Equal quantities of pork, veal and beef suet are minced and mixed with breadcrumbs, herbs, lemon rind and seasoning. The mixture is shaped into sausages on a well-floured board. These are dipped in egg, then breadcrumbs, and fried in hot fat till golden.

RESTAURANTS & HOTELS

We would like to thank the following for their help and generosity in giving us the recipes listed below. Oxford telephone numbers and opening times are also provided.

BROWNS RESTAURANT, 5-9 Woodstock Road 511995
Chef: G. Strivens
Steak, Guinness and mushroom pie, 22
Peasants' pots, 28
Banana cheesecake, 46
Open: 11 am-11 pm

ISIS HOTEL, 45-53 Iffley Road 48894
Cook Jane Lodge
Trout Isis, 39
Old-fashioned fruit pudding, 48
Luncheon: 12-2 pm. Dinner: 7-8.30 pm

LA CANTINA DI CAPRI, 34 Queen Street 47760
Chef/proprietor: Reno Pizi
Veal Reno, 26
Chicken Veronica, 31
Luncheon: 12-2.30 pm. Dinner: 6-11.30 pm (Tues-Sat)

LADBROKE LINTON LODGE, 11-13 Linton Road 53461
Chef: Raymond Killick
Chicken and walnut pâté, 13
Cherwell cutlets, 29
Linton Lodge syllabub, 50
Dinner: 7-9.30 pm

LA SORBONNE RESTAURANT, 130A High Street 41320
Chef de cuisine/proprietor: André Chavagnon
L'aiguillette de canard sauvage a l'Armagnac, 34
Luncheon: 12-2.30 pm. Dinner: 7-11 pm

LES QUAT' SAISONS RESTAURANT 53540
272 Banbury Road, Summertown
Chef/proprietor: R. R. A. Blanc
Gâteau de topinambours au coulis d'asperges, 14
Salade de caille, 36
Coquilles St Jacques à la julienne de légumes, 38
Luncheon: 12-2 pm. Dinner: 7.15-10 pm (Tues-Sat)

MUNCHY MUNCHY, 6 Park End Street 45710
Chefs/proprietors: Tony and Ethel Ow
Rojak, 11; Saté-udang, 15
Malaysian hamburgers, 23; Kerepek pisang, 55
Luncheon: 12-2.30 pm (Tues-Sat)
Dinner: 5.30-10 pm (Tues-Sat)

MAISON BLANC PATISSERIE 50974
3 Woodstock Road
Proprietors: M. and Mme Blanc
Charlotte aux fraises, 47
Gâteau citron, 54
Open: 7.30 am-6 pm (Mon-Sat)

THE NOSEBAG, 6-8 St Michael's Street 721033
Cooks: Sarah Woodley and Gay Jennings
Nosebag salad, 13
Banana bread, 58
Open: 10 am-5.30 pm (Mon-Sat). 6.30-9-30 pm (Fri-Sat). 12-5.30 pm (Sun)

THE OLD PARSONAGE HOTEL, 1-3 Banbury Road 54843
Chef: Brett Masters
Parsonage golden steak, 23
Dinner: 7 pm-9 pm. Luncheon: 12.30-2 pm (Sun)

THE OPIUM DEN, 79 George Street 48680
Chef: Alan Tse
Sweet and sour pork, 27
Lemon chicken Cantonese style, 32
Luncheon: 12-2.30 pm (Sun: 1-2.30 pm)
Dinner: 6-midnight

RANDOLPH HOTEL, Beaumont Street 47481
Chefs: Mick Maguire (Head chef)
Timothy Edmonds (Sous chef)
Frogs' legs with sour cream and chives, 18
Quail with green peppercorns, 35
Baked sea bass, 39
Chilled almond soufflé, 53
Luncheon: 12.30-2.15 pm. Dinner: 7-10.15 pm

RESTAURANT ELIZABETH, 84 St Aldates 42230
Proprietor: Senor Lopez
Rice in paella, 42
Luncheon: 12.30-2.30 (Sun)
Dinner: 6.30-11 pm (Tues-Sat). 7-10.30 pm (Sun)

SARACENO RESTAURANT, 15 Magdalen Street 49171
Chef: Giovanni Ventriglia
Petti di pollo reale, 33
Zabaglione al Marsala, 47
Luncheon: 12.30-2.30 pm. 7-11.30 pm (Mon-Sat)

TURF TAVERN, 4-5 Bath Place 43235
Chef: Sally Smith
Upside-down pear pudding, 52
Turf's special dessert, 55
Luncheon: 11.45-2.15 pm. 12-1.50 pm (Sun)
Dinner: 6-9.30 pm

WRENS, 29 Castle Street 42944
Chef/proprietor: J. Geoghegan
Paupiettes de sole St Pierre, 16
Terrine de trois poissons au beurre blanc, 17
Poulet en pot à la Marengo, 32
Mosaique de poissons Marseillaise, 37
Profiteroles à ma facon, 50
Prune and port meringue pie, 54
Omelette Normande, 58
Dinner: 7-10.30 pm (Mon-Sat)

ONE LAST SPOONFUL!
REV W.A. Spooner, Warden of New College, gave his name to the "spoonerism", in which two letters are transposed. *"Sir, you have tasted two whole worms; you have hissed all the mystery lectures and been caught fighting a liar in the quad; you will leave Oxford by the next town drain."* (A student who has wasted two terms, missed his history lectures and lit a fire in the quad, was sent down — expelled — and told to catch the down train to London!)

TIME TO LEAVE . . .
Most students are not sent down! But when exams are over, and the time has come for them to leave the University, they celebrate in style.

"Let us drink to the queer old Dean!"
DR SPOONER'S famous toast to Queen Victoria.

We reluctantly left Oxford in our search for other centres of culinary excellence. Look out for other books in this series on your travels.

Available now:
The Bath Cookbook
The Cambridge Cookbook
The Oxford Cookbook
The Stratford Cookbook

In preparation:
The Cotswolds Cookbook
The Edinburgh Cookbook
The Thames Cookbook
The York Cookbook